THE VISUAL GUIDE
BY SCOTT BEATTY

BATMAN CREATED BY BOB KANE

LONDON, NEW YORK, MUNICH,
MELBOURNE AND DELHI

Project Editor Catherine Saunders
Senior Designer Robert Perry
Publishing Manager Simon Beecroft
Publisher Alex Allan
Art Director Mark Richards
Production Lloyd Robertson
DTP Designer Lauren Egan

05 06 07 08 09 10 9 8 7 6 5 4 3 2 1

First published in Great Britain in 2005 by
Dorling Kindersley Ltd,
80 Strand, London WC2R 0RL
A Penguin Company

A catalogue record for this book is available from the British Library.

ISBN 1-4053-1003-0

Colour reproduction by Media Development and Printing Ltd., UK
Printed and bound in Italy by L.E.G.O.

Visit DC Comics online at www.dccomics.com
or at keyword DC Comics on America Online

Discover more at
www.dk.com

CONTENTS

Foreword by Dennis O'Neil   6

The Wayne Family   8

Bruce Takes a Fall   10

A Night at the Opera   12

Murder!   14

No Justice   16

Lost Soul   18

The Journey   20

Rā's al Ghūl   22

The League of Shadows   24

The Final Test   26

Return to Gotham   28

The Criminal Element   30

Wayne Enterprises   32

The Batcave   34

Creating the Bat   36

The Batsuit   38

Tools of the Trade   40

The Tumbler   42

The Batmobile   44

Bruce Wayne: Billionaire   46

Fighting Back   48

The Scarecrow   50

Fear Factor   52

Batman to the Rescue   54

Birthday Party   56

Terror in the Narrows   58

Batman Wins   60

The Fight Continues   62

Acknowledgements   64

FOREWORD

BY DENNIS O'NEIL

Batman has been entertaining and exciting audiences for over 65 years now, but he hasn't done it resting on his laurels. During his long career as a pop culture icon, he's done a lot of evolving: he's been a wealthy dilettante who fought crime almost as a hobby, a disembodied voice on the radio, a cheery role model, a darkly obsessed avenger, and – the most enduring version – a man who turned tragedy into a vocation and, in the process, perfected himself. Each incarnation had its merits and each was appropriate to its era, which might help explain Batman's longevity.

Throughout all of Batman's incarnations there has been one constant – Batman has great crime-fighting tools. Batman's various gadgets have sprung from the imaginations and craftsmanship of generations of creative men and women, beginning with Bob Kane and Bill Finger, who began the Batman saga back in 1939, through the comics writers and artists who followed them and on to the designers and art directors who contributed to Batman's various film and television incarnations. Our hero's props have always been a part of what makes the character enjoyable, as have the gothic cityscapes in which he and his friends and foes lurk. The latest versions of both Batman's crime-fighting technology and his urban environment were developed for the movie *Batman Begins* and are presented in the pages that follow. Some are strikingly contemporary reinventions of old favorites and some are nifty new stuff inspired by what's cutting-edge in both Batman's world and our own.

For Batman, these items are tools. For us, they're a lot of fun to look at and ponder, and they bring us deeper into the realm of Batman, which is what this book is all about.

For more than 20 years, Batman editor and writer
Dennis O'Neil has put the "dark" in the Dark Knight and
has been a guiding force behind the Batman mythos.

THE WAYNE FAMILY

"Gotham's been good to our family..."

Judge Solomon Wayne declared more than a century ago that Gotham City should be a "fortress against vice and iniquity", and no other name is more closely associated with the rise of Gotham than that of the Wayne family. Viewed as the city's "First Family", the Waynes' considerable fortune brought commerce and industry to the developing city. Wayne Manor was by default Gotham's castle-keep, watching over the city from its high perch. As the family profited from the city's continued expansion, the Waynes in turn gave generously to the citizens of Gotham. Unfortunately, like all great dynasties, the Waynes face an uncertain and troubled future.

THE LUXURY of Wayne Manor is in stark contrast to the rest of Gotham. Despite the many contributions the Waynes have made to prop up the city's stagnating economy, it is rife with unemployment and crime.

THE HISTORY OF WAYNE MANOR

The stately Wayne family residence started out as the home of Gotham railway financier Jerome K. van Derm, who broke ground on the Manor in 1855. Not long after the mansion's completion, van Derm's land ventures failed, forcing him to relinquish the deed. Even then it was a prime location, at the centre of more than 300 wooded acres overlooking, yet some distance removed from, Gotham City. Brothers Solomon and Zebediah Wayne took possession of the mansion in 1858 and Solomon commissioned the often-maligned Gothic architect Cyrus Pinkney to expand Wayne Manor into its present structure. It remains the heart of the Wayne family's empire nearly 150 years later.

LIGHT AND SPACE

The grandeur of Wayne Manor belies a famously cold and draughty interior. This is largely due to a vast, secret network of limestone caverns which run underneath the whole estate. During her time as lady of the house, Martha Wayne took it upon herself to drive out the damp and darkness with warm furnishings and a constant supply of fresh flowers from the Manor's own greenhouse.

MANY OF the antiques which grace the rooms of Wayne Manor have been in the family for generations, while others have been collected by Thomas Wayne during working holidays abroad. The hand-turned mahogany furniture in Thomas and Martha's sitting room began life as trees on Wayne plantations in Belize.

THOMAS AND MARTHA WAYNE

THOMAS WAYNE

They were a perfect match. Thomas Wayne had long admired his neighbour Martha Kane, heiress to the Kane Chemical dynasty, and Martha had no time for the spoilt rich boys who usually tried to date her. Society tongues wagged when it was announced that the recently graduated Dr Thomas Wayne, heir to an even larger fortune, had asked for Martha's hand in marriage. After what was surely Gotham's grandest wedding and a honeymoon to parts unknown – in avoidance of paparazzi – the Waynes set about using their combined wealth for the betterment of Gotham. Although a well-known patron of the arts, Martha was also a

driving force behind raising funds for Gotham's poor. And for his part, Thomas Wayne left the day-to-day running of Wayne Enterprises to "better men", while he offered his surgical skills pro bono to Gotham University Hospital and other city medical centres.

MARTHA WAYNE

BRUCE TAKES A FALL

"And why do we fall, Master Bruce?"

Bruce and his friend Rachel Dawes loved to play in Wayne Manor's extensive grounds. But one fateful day, their childish game went badly wrong. As Bruce scrambled over an abandoned well, the rotten boards splintered and he fell more than 9 metres (30 feet). In the darkness below, Bruce discovered that he had fallen into the vast underground cave system beneath Wayne Manor. As he lay there, injured and frightened, Bruce came face to face with the most terrifying creatures he could ever imagine.

INTO THE CAVE

Upon cornering Rachel in the Manor's greenhouse, Bruce snatched the arrowhead from her grasp and ran off. With Rachel in hot pursuit, Bruce climbed into the well, a perfect hiding place during their frequent games of hide-and-seek. Except this time, the rotten boards groaned and gave way.

FINDERS KEEPERS! When Rachel found a dusty flint arrowhead on the Manor grounds, Bruce argued that since the arrowhead was found on his property, it rightfully belonged to him. Rachel disagreed and claimed, "finders keepers!"

Deep below, Bruce lay in darkness but he was not alone. From a crack in the cave wall came a swarm of bats, surrounding Bruce in an explosive flurry of teeth and claws and wings, nearly frightening him out of his wits.

ALFRED PENNYWORTH

The Wayne Family's personal valet since before Bruce was born, Alfred Pennyworth maintains that he comes from a long and distinguished line of menservants in his native England. However, Alfred's skills at acting and vocal mimicry hint at a background in the London stage. Only Bruce knows that Alfred once served Queen and country first as a medic in the British Infantry, and later as an operative for the secret service MI5. More important to Bruce, Alfred stood by his side after Bruce's parents were murdered, bringing him up as best he could but without ever attempting to replace Bruce's beloved father and mother. Alfred ultimately enables Bruce to become the Dark Knight, firstly by maintaining Wayne Manor in his absence so that Bruce would have a home to come back to after his long sojourn abroad. And secondly, by helping Bruce to create his costumed alter ego, inspired by that long ago fall into the cave. Without Alfred Pennyworth, there would be no Batman.

TIME FOR TEA

SAVED!

With Alfred anchoring the rope above, Bruce's father lowered himself into the well. Dr Wayne carried Bruce to the Manor and set his broken bones himself, reassuring Bruce's mother, that the boy was more frightened than hurt from his tumble. Later, Thomas comforted his injured son. "And why do we fall?" he said, then answering his own question, "So that we might better learn to pick ourselves up."

RACHEL'S MOTHER, Mrs Dawes, had tended Wayne Manor for many years. The two children grew up together and attended the same private primary school – with Rachel's tuition paid for by the ever-generous Waynes.

THE NECKLACE was a string of flawless pearls, a gift from Thomas Wayne to his wife Martha. To Bruce, it was a secret shared between father and son and a welcome distraction from the nightmares that haunted him following his close encounter with the bats.

A NIGHT AT THE OPERA

"A bit of opera goes a long way…"

If he had the choice, Bruce would have preferred to attend a showing of *The Mark of Zorro* at Gotham's dilapidated Regal Cinema but his mother, looking splendid in her new pearl necklace, favoured "higher art", especially the opera. Bruce had promised his parents that he wouldn't fidget in his seat or fiddle with his uncomfortably formal suit and tie during the performance. But when the curtain rose on Arrigo Boito's *Mefistofle* and Bruce witnessed the spectacle of Faust's supernatural temptations, he relived his own recent descent into a cavernous underworld populated by nightmarish creatures.

FAMILY OUTING

The wealthy Wayne family were often to be seen out at the Gotham City Opera House as Martha Wayne attempted to introduce her son to more cultured forms of entertainment than his beloved old movie serials. But tonight, as the hellish creatures cavorted on stage, Bruce's breathing became laboured and a familiar panic gripped him.

MEFISTOFLE or Mephistopheles is another name for Satan and the opera is a musical retelling of Faust's ultimate redemption and defeat of Satan.
Had Bruce known the opera ended happily, he might have been able to stifle his fears of the devilish creatures on stage. But all he could see were bats.

UNDERSTANDING Bruce's fear, Thomas Wayne quietly ushered his family out of the theatre by a side door. None of them realized the terrible fate that awaited them as they left the opera house.

MURDER!

"I said the jewellery!"

The side exit to the theatre was in a dingy back alley, strewn with litter. But henceforth it would be known as "Crime Alley". It was to be the scene of the most infamous crime in Gotham's history. Had the Waynes not departed the opera early, their limousine would have picked them up at the front of the theatre but Thomas and Martha decided to take in the cool night air, to calm Bruce after his panic attack. They should have known better. The streets of Gotham were no place for the defenceless, especially after sunset.

CRIME ALLEY became symbolic of the moral decay in Gotham City. Later in life, Bruce Wayne made pilgrimages to the spot where his father and mother were cruelly taken from him, leaving flowers to honour their memory.

BRUCE'S BALEFUL gaze forced Chill to turn and flee, leaving the boy as sole survivor and lone witness to the murders.

A DESPERATE MAN

Joe Chill was one of countless people left destitute by the city's economic depression. Laid off from his less-than-minimum wage job on the docks, Chill turned to alcohol. A bottle fuelled his courage when he bought a pistol and roamed the streets for people to rob. Nevertheless, Chill's hand shook as he attempted to mug the Waynes. Chill ordered Dr Wayne to hand over his wallet and, for the sake of his family, Thomas complied.

MARTHA'S pearls caught Chill's eye and he lunged for them. As Thomas stepped protectively in front of his wife, Chill fired. To silence Martha's screams, Chill fired again. And again. The Waynes didn't stand a chance.

ALL ALONE

Bruce was just ten years old when he was orphaned by Joe Chill's bullets. Life would never be the same for him. But Thomas Wayne had prepared for the eventuality of his and Martha's untimely deaths and legal guardianship of Bruce was granted to Alfred Pennyworth. With her employers gone, Mrs Dawes sought other employment. Bruce and Rachel remained close, yet their friendship was never quite the same as Bruce grew to manhood in the cold and lonely mansion.

THOMAS AND MARTHA were laid to rest in the grounds of Wayne Manor. They joined previous generations of Waynes interred at the foot of a grand old oak tree planted by Alan Wayne, the only son of Judge Solomon Wayne.

WILLIAM EARLE paid his respects to the orphaned Bruce at the Waynes' funeral. As newly installed Chief Executive Officer of Wayne Enterprises, Earle assured Bruce that he would look after Wayne Enterprises on his behalf.

ALFRED knew that Bruce blamed himself for the death of his parents. If it wasn't for his fear the family would never have been in Crime Alley. Alfred comforted Bruce in the months that followed, reassuring the distraught boy that the tragedy was not his fault.

15

NO JUSTICE

"Someone should stand for my parents."

Joe Chill was picked up by the G.C.P.D. just hours after he shot Thomas and Martha Wayne and left them to die on the cracked pavement of Crime Alley. Chill even had the murder weapon in his shaking hands, ready to drop it into a sewer grate as the cops closed in. Ballistics reports linked Chill's gun to the bullets found in the Waynes' bodies. A jury of twelve men and women, moved by young Bruce Wayne's tearful testimony, had no hesitation in sentencing Chill to life in Blackgate Penitentiary, without reprieve. But for Bruce Wayne, there could be no restitution for the killing of his parents.

HAUNTED BY the memory of his beloved parents, Bruce planned to kill Chill at the parole hearing.

CHILL MAKES PAROLE

In Blackgate, Chill shared a cell with mob boss Carmine Falcone. Falcone confessed everything to his cellmate, believing that Chill was as unrepentant a criminal as himself. Little did Falcone know that Chill had cut a deal with the District Attorney and was willing to testify against him in exchange for early release from prison. After just fourteen years behind bars, Chill would be a free man.

CHILL claimed that prison had rehabilitated him and that he felt remorse.

WHILE BRUCE spent the last few years getting kicked out of nearly the entire Ivy League, Rachel devoted herself to her studies, graduating with distinction from Gotham University. Rachel's faith in the legal system led her to law school and from there to an internship at the District Attorney's office. She fervently believed that Gotham could be changed for the better if good people stood up against crime and corruption.

FALCONE DECIDES

The parole board unanimously granted Joe Chill his freedom but Judge Faden and at least one other board member were on Falcone's payroll. Falcone arranged for Chill to be escorted from the court and into a trap. As a throng of eager reporters surrounded him, Chill's guard was down, especially for one pretty blonde. In a split second she denied Bruce the revenge he so desperately sought.

THE ASSASSIN distracted Chill with a microphone in her right hand while pulling a pistol and firing on him with her left!

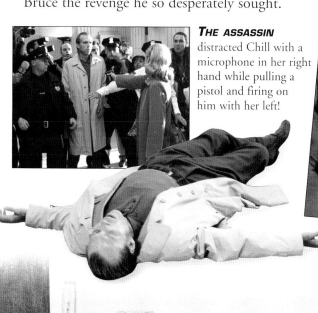

FEELING CHEATED, Bruce confronted Falcone at his club. With Judge Faden looking on, Falcone pistol-whipped Bruce and educated him on the nature of fear and power, reminding Bruce just how far his influence stretched in Gotham. It was a lesson Bruce would never forget.

THE JOURNEY BEGINS

Tossing away his wallet and trading his expensive coat for a threadbare one worn by a homeless man, Bruce abandoned his old life. Bruce took the first ship out of Gotham, not knowing when he might return. For all intents and purposes, Bruce Wayne was missing, presumed dead.

LOST SOUL

Bruce wasn't sure of his destination when he stowed away on a cargo ship as it steamed out of Gotham Harbor. His goal was to learn the kind of things he couldn't find in books, but rather on the backstreets of foreign cities where no one knew – or cared – who he was. He wanted to know how to hunt, how to fight, how to survive. His teachers weren't learned scholars; in fact most were wanted men. But from them, Bruce would finally understand the criminal mind and in doing so, he would at last conquer his fear.

JAILBIRD

From pickpockets and carjackers to thieves and con men, Bruce observed firsthand how the criminal mind worked. He learned that some people commit crimes out of necessity, others out of greed or malice. When double-crossed during a warehouse heist in Shanghai, Bruce made no attempt to reveal his identity to the police or the court that sentenced him to twenty years in prison, although the only person he had robbed was himself!

擎德監獄

BADGE OF THE CHINESE
PRISON AUTHORITIES

FROM HIS cellmate, an old man who had served a nearly a lifetime behind bars, Bruce realized that his punishment might well have been a death sentence.

EVER SINCE he walked through the prison gates, Bruce had been accosted daily by other inmates as he lined up in the courtyard for the prisoners' one and only meal of the day – a bowl of thin gruel. One of them, probably the biggest man Bruce had ever seen, would never leave the prison for throttling to death a dozen peasants with his bare hands. For sport, he picked a fight with Bruce.

IN A FAIR FIGHT Bruce would have battled his aggressor one-on-one. Instead, five other prisoners made it a brawl. While the others had no personal grudge against Bruce, it seemed that someone else had given them an incentive to test Bruce's mettle in unarmed combat.

STARTING WITH the biggest, Bruce bested every single one of his opponents. After shattering the giant's kneecap with a foot-sweep, Bruce took the fight out of him by mashing his nose to pulp with his boot. Bruce made short work of his other attackers, breaking bones and mixing blood with the prison mud.

MACHINE GUN FIRE ended the melee as one of the guards shot into the air to scatter the crowd who had gathered to watch the brawl. Bruce was dragged away to solitary confinement – to protect the other inmates!

SOLITARY CONFINEMENT

In solitary confinement Bruce found Henri Ducard, a free man with considerable influence within the walls of the prison. Ducard seemed to know a lot about Bruce and his journey. Speaking for his master, Rā's al Ghūl, leader of the League of Shadows, he offered Bruce a new path, and a chance to become "more than a man". Bruce felt that he had nothing to lose and much to gain from the offer.

DUCARD PROMISED Bruce early release from prison, and the guards delivered him to the foothills of the Himalayas to continue his journey.

A **HIMALAYAN PLATEAU** offered little nourishment for the hungry and weary Bruce. Edible lichens and moss provided him with just enough energy to continue onwards and upwards.

THE JOURNEY

"To conquer fear, you must become fear."

Ducard's challenge was simple: On the Eastern slopes of Tibet's Himalayan range grew a rare blue poppy; if Bruce was serious about serving true justice then he need only pick a single flower and carry it up the mountain. Then, and only then, would he find what he was seeking – the path to becoming more than a man. With just the clothes on his back, including the threadbare coat he had worn since leaving Gotham, Bruce began his ascent into the unknown. He had a small satchel of food and water, barely enough sustenance for the forbidding and unforgiving environment that loomed before him.

BLUE POPPIES thrive in harsh landscapes and only grow between 3000 and 4000 metres (10,000 and 13,000 feet).

NO TURNING BACK

The further he climbed, the closer Bruce came to death, his belly knotted in hunger and his extremities nipped by frostbite. In the thin air of high altitude, a delirious Bruce was driven on by sheer force of will. If he really was lost and in need of a path to follow, then surely it must lie at the top of the mountain as Ducard promised. He had gone past the point of no return a long time ago. Where else could he go?

PRAYER FLAGS are planted by Tibetan Buddhists to carry harmonious vibrations on the winds and ensure happiness and prosperity for travellers, like Bruce.

AT THE VERY TOP of the mountain, a tired Bruce discovered an ancient monastery, a grand wooden structure rising majestically from the rock and snow. As Bruce pounded on the monastery's doors with all his might, exhaustion finally overwhelmed him. Would he find the answers Ducard promised inside?

RĀ'S AL GHŪL
"Make no mistake, here you face death."

Bruce had heard rumours of the League of Shadows and its enigmatic master during his travels. Now, helpless and exhausted, he stood before the warrior leader, Rā's al Ghūl, as Ducard translated his master's words. Reputedly immortal, Rā's al Ghūl was a man whose very presence commanded respect, and inspired fear. Bruce had nowhere else to go: Rā's al Ghūl would now decide if he lived or died.

BRUCE TOLD Rā's al Ghūl that he sought the means to fight injustice and to turn fear against those who prey on the fearful. As Ducard translated, Rā's replied "To manipulate the fears of others, you must first master your own."

SAVIOUR OR DESTROYER

Rā's al Ghūl is believed to have been born several hundred years ago in North Africa. As a child, it was foretold that he would become the world's saviour, or its destroyer. He became a self-appointed messiah who used his influence to advise kings and despots so that their actions would ultimately benefit his plan to return Earth to an Eden-like state of grace. Although Rā's al Ghūl is believed to have sired hundreds of children, only two were sons and as they died in infancy he still seeks a male heir to his great legacy.

THE BLUE POPPY

From the folds of his tattered and torn coat, Bruce produced the blue poppy that he had carried up the mountain, just as Ducard had instructed. Despite the long and arduous climb during which Bruce nearly tumbled down the steep slope to his death, the flower was intact. Now it was currency, the single item that would grant Bruce safe passage within the monastery.

A NEW DISCIPLE: Bruce accepted Rā's al Ghūl's challenge, but first he needed to rest after his long journey. Unfortunately, Ducard had other plans – Bruce's training had begun.

SURPRISE ATTACK! To test Bruce's resolve, Ducard kicked the exhausted Bruce to the floor of the monastery. "Death does not wait for you to be ready."

FIGHTING MASTER

Ducard was an expert swordsman, easily besting Bruce at every turn with his ninja katana.

TRAINING

Ducard began honing Bruce's fighting skills. Before his incarceration, Bruce had mastered more than a dozen martial arts, and Ducard was much impressed with Bruce's skills in ju-jitsu and swordplay. But as he pointed out to Bruce, fighting is not a dance. Bruce must be mindful of his surroundings and more importantly, he must control his anger.

BRUCE DISARMED Ducard on the ice but then allowed himself to be fooled by Ducard's feint. Intent on defeating his teacher, the pupil failed to notice the ice cracking beneath his feet. A plunge into freezing water cooled Bruce's temper.

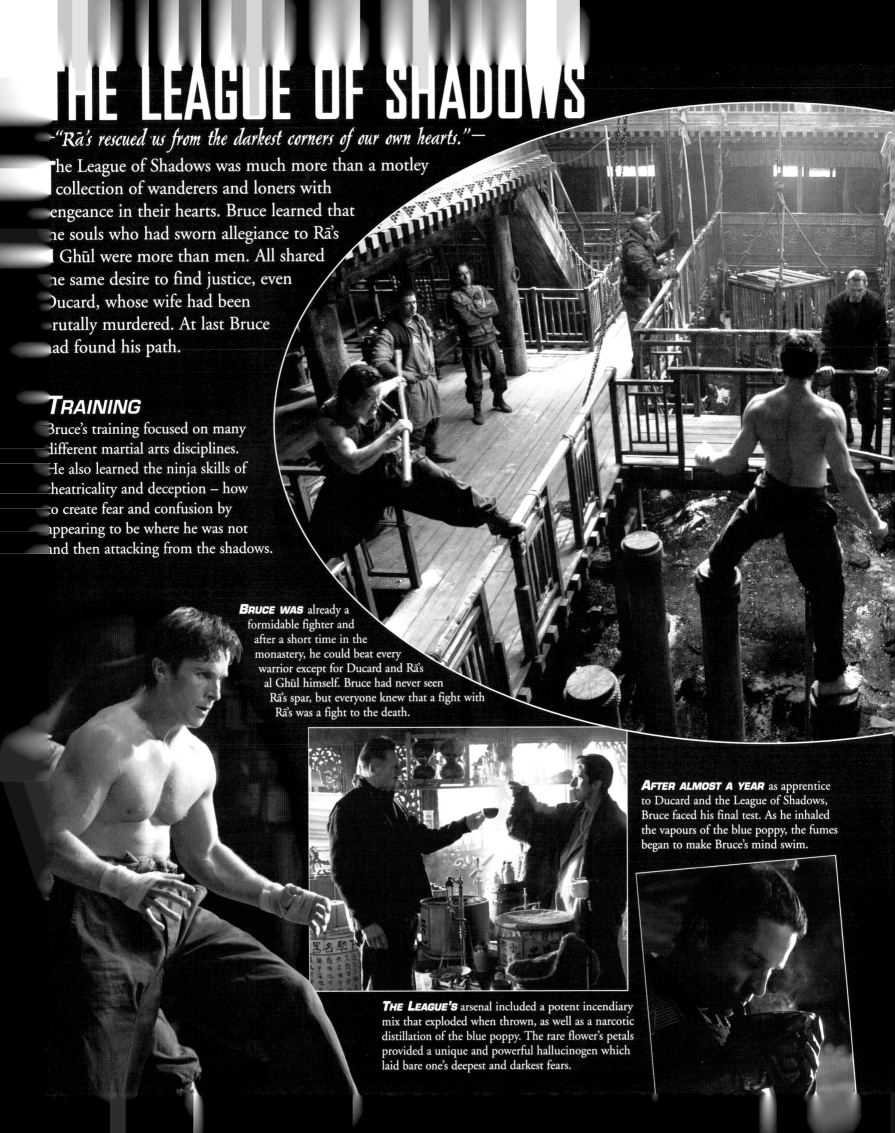

THE LEAGUE OF SHADOWS

—"Rā's rescued us from the darkest corners of our own hearts."—

The League of Shadows was much more than a motley collection of wanderers and loners with vengeance in their hearts. Bruce learned that the souls who had sworn allegiance to Rā's al Ghūl were more than men. All shared the same desire to find justice, even Ducard, whose wife had been brutally murdered. At last Bruce had found his path.

TRAINING

Bruce's training focused on many different martial arts disciplines. He also learned the ninja skills of theatricality and deception – how to create fear and confusion by appearing to be where he was not and then attacking from the shadows.

BRUCE WAS already a formidable fighter and after a short time in the monastery, he could beat every warrior except for Ducard and Rā's al Ghūl himself. Bruce had never seen Rā's spar, but everyone knew that a fight with Rā's was a fight to the death.

AFTER ALMOST A YEAR as apprentice to Ducard and the League of Shadows, Bruce faced his final test. As he inhaled the vapours of the blue poppy, the fumes began to make Bruce's mind swim.

THE LEAGUE'S arsenal included a potent incendiary mix that exploded when thrown, as well as a narcotic distillation of the blue poppy. The rare flower's petals provided a unique and powerful hallucinogen which laid bare one's deepest and darkest fears.

HISTORY OF THE LEAGUE

Rā's al Ghūl is committed to restoring Earth to paradise and he created the League of Shadows to help him further that end. The League has acted at crucial points in global history, from the sacking of Rome to the Great Fire of London. The League of Shadows is Rā's al Ghūl's army, and each man knows that he is expendable, his life forfeit, if it means fulfillment of Rā's al Ghūl's ultimate plans. Like Bruce, each Shadow fighter hungers for vengeance to redress a crime inflicted upon him or his loved ones. Rā's uses this to his advantage, promising his warriors retribution on a global scale. The League have influenced the destiny of mankind for several centuries but Rā's al Ghūl's reasons remain a mystery. An immortal can afford to be patient.

THE WARRIORS line up to swear allegiance to Rā's al Ghūl and promise to uphold the code of the League of Shadows.

TESTED TO THE LIMIT

Reeling from the powerful hallucinogen and surrounded by the League's warriors, Bruce was ordered to open a wooden box. Inside, he found a swarm of bats. But the bats could no longer terrify him – Bruce's training had worked and he had overcome his terrible fear. All that remained was to face Ducard in final combat. As Ducard slashed Bruce's sleeve, Bruce allowed himself to be swallowed up by the wall of ninjas, becoming one with the darkness.

LIKE A SHADOW, Bruce weaved amongst the ninjas, slashing several warriors' sleeves and staying a few steps ahead of Ducard. "You cannot leave any sign," Ducard taunted his apprentice as he seized a ninja with a slashed tunic.

PUPIL FINALLY DEFEATED master as Bruce revealed himself. The ninja at the edge of Ducard's blade was not Bruce Wayne but the warrior holding a sword at Ducard's neck was! Bruce had mastered the ninja arts of stealth and deception.

SHADOW WARRIOR: Bruce had proved his mettle to Rā's al Ghūl but to be fully anointed into the League of Shadows, a single test remained. Like all the other ninjas loyal to Rā's al Ghūl, Bruce would have to demonstrate his commitment to justice.

THE FINAL TEST

—"First, you must demonstrate your commitment to justice."—

For Bruce it was the final test, the culmination of all his hard work and training under Henri Ducard's expert tutelage. A murderer knelt before Rā's al Ghūl, captured by the League of Shadows. Bruce's membership of the League and his worth as a ninja hinged on completion of a single task – he must execute the murderer. As the murderer desperately pleaded for his life, Bruce contemplated his future.

CRISIS OF CONSCIENCE

Bruce refused to be the League's executioner. The League of Shadows had taught him an unexpected lesson; he could not kill the defenceless man. Bruce was no longer the angry young man who had planned revenge on Joe Chill. As Rā's al Ghūl mocked Bruce's compassion, Bruce learned the League's plans for him – he was to join them in destroying Gotham City, a breeding ground for suffering and injustice that Rā's al Ghūl considered well beyond saving.

RĀ'S ATTACKED as Bruce hit Ducard with the flat of his sword to take the fight out of at least one foe. The League's enigmatic leader unsheathed his own sword, prepared to slay Bruce if he would not swear allegiance to him.

FIRE! Bruce struck a ceremonial brazier, sending hot coals flying towards the League's supply of powdered incendiaries. Ninjas were tossed like rag dolls as explosions rocked the interior and Bruce and Rā's al Ghūl finally crossed swords.

THE MONASTERY'S destruction took very little time. Determined to run through Bruce with his sword, Rā's al Ghūl failed to notice the flaming timbers above him. As Rā's al Ghūl was lost in a crash of fiery debris, Bruce hoisted the unconscious Ducard onto his shoulders and leapt out of a crumbling balcony while the monastery disintegrated in a final blazing fireball.

THRUSTING the bronze gauntlet into the rock and snow, Bruce halted their slide just in time, as Ducard dangled over the perilous drop below.

SAVING DUCARD

Despite Ducard's loyalties to Rā's al Ghūl, Bruce felt a strange kinship with his mentor. Ducard had spoken hard truths, but he seemed to understand Bruce's need for justice. Unfortunately, Bruce's haste to save Ducard almost doomed them both. Propelled down the mountain by the force of the blast, Bruce and the unconscious Ducard tumbled right towards the edge of a cliff and nothing but a fatal fall beyond! Only Bruce's quick reactions saved them from oblivion.

AT THE FOOT of the mountain, Bruce left Ducard in the care of an old man who he had met on his way up the mountain to the monastery.

FLYING HOME aboard a Wayne Enterprises jet waiting for him in Kathmandu, Bruce greeted Alfred for the first time in seven years. Bruce was ready to return to home. His training was complete and the war on crime could begin.

RETURN TO GOTHAM

"This city is rotting."

Bruce returns to a Gotham City that has descended even further into ruin. As he flies over the city, Bruce sees Wayne Tower gleaming in the heart of Midtown, but elsewhere the city's worsening economic depression is obvious. As Gotham's economy flounders, unemployment is at an all-time high and crime and vice run rampant. Bruce's parents would hardly recognize the city they loved and tried so hard to improve. But Bruce aims to change that – he has returned with a sense of purpose.

BACK HOME, Bruce has Alfred to thank for looking after the manor.

DECAYING CITY

It is a known fact that unemployment and poverty lead to a rising crime rate as the poor steal to survive. Quality of life diminishes as alcohol and drug abuse increase among a population seeking to drown its sorrows. Nowhere is this more apparent than in Gotham. Today the city that once prided itself on its unique architecture and rich history, on its industry and innovation, is rotting to its core. Graffiti defaces the crumbling buildings, litter clogs the streets, and the citizens are choked by apathy and despair.

THE NARROWS were built to connect industrial Downtown Gotham to corporate Midtown and to provide low-cost housing for the poor. Originally salt marshes, the land was drained and joined to the other islands by nine bridges. Wayne Enterprises helped to build low-cost tenements but after the death of Thomas Wayne, the buildings were left to the care of its tenants and fell into disrepair. Crosstown bridges were later built to bypass this area.

DRESSED AS a homeless person, Bruce surveys Gotham's mean streets, observing the corruption and crime. He also keeps a watchful eye over his childhood friend Rachel Dawes, discovering that she has much to fear from Carmine Falcone's henchmen.

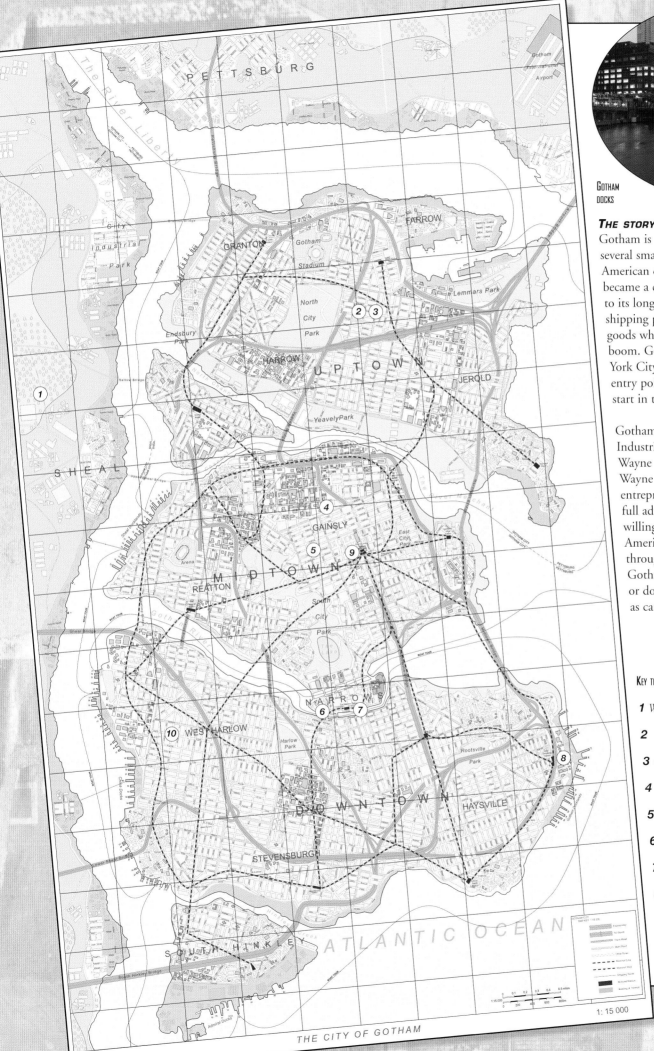

THE STORY OF GOTHAM

Gotham is comprised of three large islands and several smaller ones. Like many Northeastern American cities in the 19th century, Gotham became a centre for industrialization. Thanks to its long coastline, it became a major shipping port for imported and exported goods which in turn fuelled the industrial boom. Gotham was also second only to New York City and its celebrated Ellis Island as an entry point for immigrants seeking a fresh start in the United States.

Gotham itself grew rapidly during the Industrial Revolution with companies like Wayne Manufacturing (soon to become Wayne Enterprises) and other entrepreneurially minded ventures taking full advantage of enthusiastic citizens willing to work hard to achieve the American Dream. But unfortunately throughout every economic boom in Gotham's history the inevitable recession or downturn has never been far behind, as can be seen in the city's present state.

KEY TO MAP

1 *Wayne Manor*

2 *Gotham Opera House*

3 *Crime Alley*

4 *G.C.P.D. Headquarters*

5 *Gotham Municipal Courthouse*

6 *The Narrows*

7 *Arkham Asylum*

8 *Falcone's club*

9 *Wayne Tower*

10 *Rachel Dawes' apartment*

THE CITY OF GOTHAM

THE CRIMINAL ELEMENT

"This is a world you'll never understand."

Gotham City is rotten to the core thanks to people like Carmine Falcone. Falcone's influence extends from the lowly street cop paid to look the other way to high-ranking city officials pulling strings for the mob to satisfy their greed for money and power. "As long as Falcone keeps the bad people rich, and the good people scared, no one will touch him," Rachel Dawes explains to the recently returned Bruce Wayne. But little does anyone realize that they are all pawns in a darker game played from the shadows beyond Gotham.

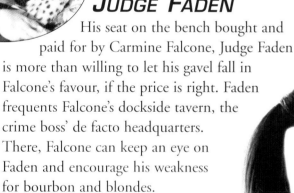

CARMINE FALCONE rules Gotham's underworld with an iron fist. Narcotics trafficking, gambling, prostitution and every conceivable illegal vice are controlled by Falcone's organization. Even rival gangs like the Odessa Mob, Escabedo Cartel and the Lucky Hand Triad concede that no crime happens in Gotham without Falcone's approval. Falcone makes sure that nothing and no one stands in his way.

JUDGE FADEN

His seat on the bench bought and paid for by Carmine Falcone, Judge Faden is more than willing to let his gavel fall in Falcone's favour, if the price is right. Faden frequents Falcone's dockside tavern, the crime boss' de facto headquarters. There, Falcone can keep an eye on Faden and encourage his weakness for bourbon and blondes.

FLASS gives dirty cops a bad name. He does little to hide the bribes and kickbacks he demands from the Gotham shopkeepers on his beat and flaunts these "extras" to his honest partner Jim Gordon. Flass is loyal to Falcone, as long as he's well paid for it.

RACHEL DAWES and her boss, District Attorney Carl Finch, are exceptions to the rule in Gotham's legal establishment – they believe in justice. Rachel and Finch assembled the case against Falcone when Joe Chill turned state's evidence against his former cellmate. But in a city like Gotham, their honesty and integrity are not welcome and many people view them as dangerous troublemakers who need to be stopped, one way or another.

ARKHAM ASYLUM

Dr Amadeus Arkham founded the Elizabeth Arkham Asylum for the Criminally Insane in 1921. Tragically, the sanatorium's very first patient was Martin "Mad Dog" Hawkins, a crazed killer who brutally murdered Arkham's wife – the asylum's namesake – and their young daughter. Nestled in the heart of the poverty-stricken Narrows, Arkham's patients see little hope outside the facility's barred windows. But for a Gotham mobster, time spent here beats a rat and cockroach-infested cell on Blackgate Island!

JONATHAN CRANE lost a lucrative teaching position at Gotham University when the board denied him tenure because of his "unorthodox" teaching methods. As administrator of Arkham, Dr Crane found the perfect place to study phobia and related psychoses with human guinea pigs.

THANKS TO Dr Crane, Mr Zsaz resides comfortably in Arkham, deemed "insane" in the court of Judge Faden. A confessed serial killer, Zsaz celebrated each of his victims by scoring a hash-mark on his own body. Dr Crane finds him a fascinating subject.

WAYNE ENTERPRISES

—"Reports of my death have been greatly exaggerated."—

As Bruce Wayne enters the boardroom of the company that bears his family name, he could have heard a pin drop. The assembled board of directors can hardly believe their eyes – the son of Thomas Wayne is alive and well, and standing right in front of them! For many, especially C.E.O. Bill Earle, Bruce's return from the dead is not a cause for celebration. Although Bruce essentially owns the company, he has no controlling interest, which suits Earle as Wayne Enterprises looks to its future viability in troubled times…

C.E.O. WILLIAM EARLE

Bill Earle was one of several vice-presidents at Wayne Enterprises in Thomas Wayne's time. After Thomas was murdered, Earle lobbied board members to support his ascension to Chief Executive Officer. Once in charge, Earle eschewed Thomas Wayne's philanthropy for more profitable ventures, especially military contracts.

CORPORATE PORTFOLIO

Wayne Enterprises is integral to the economic well-being of Gotham City. The multinational corporation's roots date back to the 19th century, when capital from Judge Solomon Wayne's property ventures was used by his heirs to fund various business speculations. First came Wayne Shipping and Wayne Textiles, the latter evolving into Wayne Chemical during the Industrial Revolution. Balancing equal parts charity and consumer-driven growth, at the turn of the century the various Wayne companies united under the Wayne Enterprises banner. In the decades that followed it became even more profitable with the additions of Wayne Industries, Wayne Pharmaceutical and WayneAir to the corporate portfolio. Today, Wayne Enterprises still employs much of Gotham's work-force despite the city's recent economic downturn.

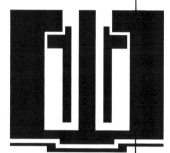

WAYNE ENTERPRISES LOGO

THE BOARD worries that Bruce will launch a hostile takeover of the company, but he assures them that is the last thing on his mind.

OVER A DRINK in Earle's office, Bruce tells the C.E.O. of his plans to become more involved with his family business. Bruce hopes to learn how Wayne Enterprises operates, one division at a time, beginning with one department in particular…

LUCIUS FOX

Lucius Fox never planned to be a businessman. In college, his aptitude for science led him to advanced studies in mechanical engineering and biochemistry but rather than becoming a research scientist, Fox was recruited to work at Wayne Industries by Thomas Wayne. Fox proved himself to be a shrewd analyst of new technology, evaluating both practical and ethical applications. Thomas and Lucius became good friends, enjoying the occasional round of golf and philosophical debates over brandy and cigars. Fox was deeply saddened when the Waynes were murdered but he was powerless to oppose Earle's takeover. Soon after, Fox was ousted from the board of directors and banished to obscurity in the Applied Sciences department.

APPLIED SCIENCES LOGO

APPLIED SCIENCES

Earle is relieved to hear of Bruce's interest in the Applied Sciences division as this dead-end department is far-removed from the important business operations. In the Applied Sciences' office, Bruce meets Lucius Fox and finds a vast storehouse of scientific and technological prototypes gathering dust. Earle thinks Bruce will quickly lose interest in Wayne Enterprises but little does he know that Bruce has very definite plans for the company's cast-offs.

FOX SHOWS Bruce several prototypes, beginning with a monofilament-firing grapnel gun. He reveals that he knew and admired Bruce's father and helped him to develop Wayne Enterprises' prized monorail system, as well as the plans to route Gotham City's water and power utilities to Wayne Tower, thus making Wayne Enterprises the unofficial heart of Gotham.

THE BATCAVE

"At least you'll have company."

Back at the Manor, Bruce sets about putting the skills he acquired during his time with the League of Shadows to the test. He prepares to revisit the place that has haunted his nightmares since childhood. Bruce understands the enormity of the task that awaits him and realizes that only the very strongest of characters can rescue Gotham from the depths of crime and iniquity to which it has sunk.

EXPLORING

Bruce descends into the Batcave the same way he did as a boy, albeit with abseiling gear for a more controlled descent this time! At first, the sheer immensity of the cave system takes his breath away. The thousands of bats blanketing the ceiling test Bruce's courage, but at last he is in control of his fear. Furthermore he has found the symbol he needs.

THE HISTORY OF THE CAVE

The cave provides not only the inspiration for Bruce's alter ego but also the perfect base to launch his crusade against crime. During the Civil War, Solomon and Joshua Wayne used the vast cavern system as an underground railway to carry Southern slaves to freedom. Now, once again, the caves will be used by a Wayne for a noble cause.

POWERING UP with a portable generator to light the cave, Bruce and Alfred install heating and ventilation. They map the cave's many tunnels, lay down a sturdier and more level concrete floor and prepare workstations for Bruce to adapt the tools of his new trade.

BRUCE FORESEES one potential flaw with his new-found base. Parking. Although its location is perfect – close to home yet cleverly concealed from the outside world – this large waterfall will make vehicular access a problem.

CREATING THE BAT

"I can't do this as Bruce Wayne."

Bruce realizes that to fight crime in Gotham, he needs to shake the city out the fear and apathy which are stifling all that is good. But he can't do it as himself – he needs to be a symbol, something incorruptible and everlasting. Despite conquering his own fear of bats, Bruce knows that the creature is a universal icon of fear and a 188 cm (6' 2") bat would certainly make the people of Gotham sit up and take notice! In the recesses of the Batcave, Bruce and Alfred set about creating Bruce's alter ego.

BRUCE BEGINS work on his costume. The bronze gauntlets he wore while a student of the League of Shadows spare him the cuts of Henri Ducard's swor more than once. Spray-painted ma black for stealth, the gauntlets a the first components of Bruce' bat costume.

BRUCE AND ALFRED

More than anyone else, Alfred Pennyworth understands Bruce's need to avenge his parents' deaths. Alfred knows there is no swaying Bruce from his vigilante crusade, so he promises to help Bruce in any way he can, especially after Bruce installs a lift to the Batcave to make the descent into darkness much smoother.

TO TEST THE mask's protective properties, Alfred takes up a baseball bat and swings it at the sculpted resin cowl. Unfortunately, the prototype model shatters into pieces, as would Bruce's skull if struck with similar force.

ALFRED AND BRUCE consult the mask's original specifications. The Kevlar lining is bulletproof, but the outer shell should also withstand blunt trauma. It turns out that there is a manufacturing problem with the graphite mixture which can be fixed.

INITIALLY BRUCE'S costume resembles the ninja gi he wore during his time with the League of Shadows. But rather than simple cloth, the Batsuit combines the modified bronze gauntlets with the Nomex survival suit and climbing harness "borrowed" from Wayne Enterprises' Applied Sciences department. Until the cowl is ready, a simple ninja mask conceals his identity.

FOX AND BAT

After researching its inventory, Bruce knows that Applied Sciences contains more than a few high-tech tools that would be invaluable to him and his crusade. Luckily, Lucius Fox is more than happy to show Bruce his abandoned prototypes. Maybe Lucius sees something beneath Bruce's playboy façade – a spark that reminds him of his late friend, Thomas Wayne.

THE COMPLETE BAT!
Two pointed ears turn the cowl mask into a truly frightening visage. The final touch is a bat-shaped insignia emblazoned across the Batsuit's chest, to make sure that everyone gets the message.

A PAINFUL fall in the Batsuit convinces Bruce that a key component is missing. He needs a bat-winged cape for a softer landing!

THE TEST FLIGHT for the scalloped cape takes place in the secrecy of the Batcave. Using the "memory fabric" supplied by Lucius Fox, Bruce passes an electrical charge through the flowing cape to turn it into a rigid glider. This time, instead of falling to the cave floor below, he glides down gracefully, like a bat.

THE BATSUIT

"…something elemental, something terrifying…"

Bruce needs a suit of armour to protect him as he wages his war on crime. This suit will strike fear into the hearts of criminals and also guard the true identity of the Dark Knight. Bruce uses every means at his disposal to outfit his alter ego for the battle to free Gotham from the grip of evil men.

PROJECT NAME
INTERNAL PROJECT NO.
CONTRACT NO.
SERIAL NO.

CNT NO. WE-36 000 PT. NO. 444-2[D]-X3

NOMEX SURVIVAL SUIT
WAYNE ENTERPRISES APPLIED SCIENCES DIVISION

LT AKIKO MANUFACTURERS

Protective cowl with Kevlar lining and tough graphite outer shell.

The cowl also conceals Bruce Wayne's features.

Batman's trademark – a symbol of his fight against injustice

Detachable cape made from "memory fabric"

WAYNE ENTERPRISES' Applied Sciences division is a treasure trove for Batman. The Batsuit began as a $300,000 Nomex survival suit for advanced infantry units. The tear-resistant Kevlar bi-weave deflects bullets, except for point blank shots and reinforced joints allow surprising freedom of movement.

Originally opaque, the Batsuit's non-reflective matte finish allows Batman to blend into shadows.

MAIL ORDERING in large quantities via a maze of untraceable shell companies provides Bruce with materials and technology not readily available through Applied Sciences.

EARPHONE

Omni-directional antenna

Digital noise reduction receiver

Shatterproof polymer aural-guard

Touch-sensitive redundant solenoid controls

Telescoping armature

Voice-activated microphone

A high-tech eavesdropping device and transmitter is concealed within the cowl's right ear. A microwave antenna enables Batman to listen in on conversations up to 1,500 metres (4,920 feet) away. It can also scan police radios, ensuring Batman is always first to the crime scene. A microphone concealed in the cowl's sculpted jaw line, allows the bat-ears to double as powerful loudspeakers, so that when Batman speaks, everyone listens!

Power link to nickel-63 micro-batteries in Batsuit

Bruce kept these bronze gauntlets from his time with the League of Shadows, spray-painting the metal matte black for camouflage.

Tempered bronze "scallops" deflect blade attacks and can also be used for climbing.

CAPE TECHNOLOGY

The material was first developed for rapid-unfolding parachute canopies used in base-jumping. The "memory fabric" becomes rigid when an electrical current is run through it, forming a pre-determined shape.

In Batman's case, the cape billows freely until he activates microcircuits in his right glove which align the fabric into a bat-winged glider, allowing him to land softly or stealthily swoop down upon his opponents.

DETAIL OF CAPE MATERIAL

Armoured calf and shin guards

Nylon-sheathed sounder in recessed heel

Steel-toed boot is both an offensive and defensive measure.

THESE BOOTS are designed to combine the flexibility of ninja tabi boots with the ruggedness of climbing shoes. Ninja climbing spikes on the Utility Belt attach easily for scaling buildings. Each heel contains a high frequency sonic "sounder" which can call bats and drive dogs crazy. When used at a lower frequency the sound makes people clutch their ears in agony.

Leather gloves packed with lead shot for added punch

Micro-relay palm and finger circuits for one-touch remote control

A HANDS-ON approach to crime-fighting, Batman's gloves are wired for remote control of the Batsuit and the Tumbler. The left glove allows for limited operation of the Tumbler from up to 3,000 metres (9,800 feet) away; the right glove controls the Batsuit.

THE WARDROBE that contains the Batsuit is secreted within the Batcave, deep beneath Wayne Manor, and includes several layers of security, including retinal-scanning digital locks to prohibit access to anyone except for Bruce or his loyal valet Alfred.

TOOLS OF THE TRADE

—"What do you want with it, Mr Wayne?"—

To Wayne Enterprises, the Applied Sciences division is more or less a storage facility for prototype technology deemed too costly for full-scale production. To Bruce Wayne, it is a ready-made arsenal for the Dark Knight. All the gadgets Bruce "borrows" from Lucius Fox exceed his expectations and offer Batman an edge over Gotham's criminal element. Augmenting the skills of theatricality and deception taught to him by Henri Ducard, these weapons will make Batman a 21st century ninja of the night.

GRAPPLING ESCAPE or swooping entrance, Batman's grapnel gun permits him the illusion of flight but with a practical application. On more than one occasion, he has used it to lift him up and out of a fight when the odds were against him. Batman is strong enough to hold the grapnel with one hand.

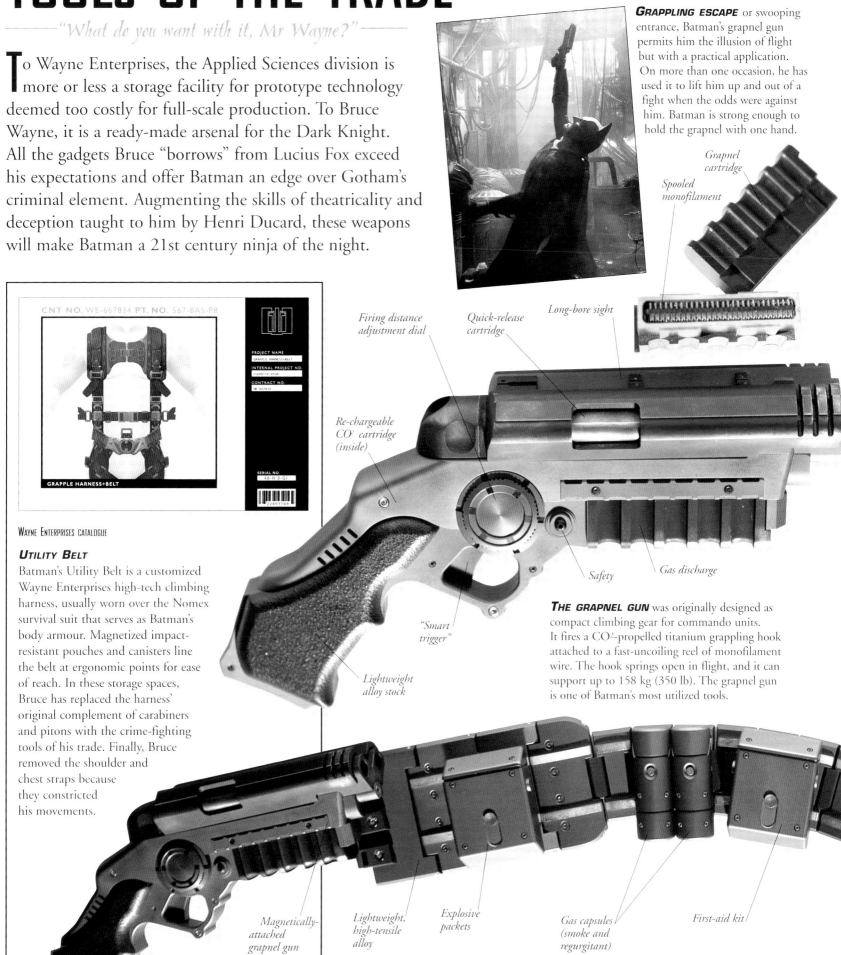

WAYNE ENTERPRISES CATALOGUE

Grapnel cartridge

Spooled monofilament

UTILITY BELT

Batman's Utility Belt is a customized Wayne Enterprises high-tech climbing harness, usually worn over the Nomex survival suit that serves as Batman's body armour. Magnetized impact-resistant pouches and canisters line the belt at ergonomic points for ease of reach. In these storage spaces, Bruce has replaced the harness' original complement of carabiners and pitons with the crime-fighting tools of his trade. Finally, Bruce removed the shoulder and chest straps because they constricted his movements.

Firing distance adjustment dial

Quick-release cartridge

Long-bore sight

Re-chargeable CO_2 cartridge (inside)

"Smart trigger"

Safety

Gas discharge

Lightweight alloy stock

THE GRAPNEL GUN was originally designed as compact climbing gear for commando units. It fires a CO_2-propelled titanium grappling hook attached to a fast-uncoiling reel of monofilament wire. The hook springs open in flight, and it can support up to 158 kg (350 lb). The grapnel gun is one of Batman's most utilized tools.

Magnetically-attached grapnel gun

Lightweight, high-tensile alloy

Explosive packets

Gas capsules (smoke and regurgitant)

First-aid kit

BATARANGS

Batman's signature weapon is an amalgam of the boomerang used by Australian Aborigines and the ninja shuriken (throwing star). Forged from high-tensile steel, Batarangs can slice through bonds, smash lights, or KO opponents swiftly and silently. These are long-distance weapons packing a steel-hard wallop!

Low gloss finish

LARGE BATARANG

LARGE BATARANG
IN BELT GRIP

SMALL BATARANG

SMALL BATARANG IN
BELT GRIP

*Spring-loaded for
fast deployment*

HAND-CRAFTED on a precision metal lathe, each Batarang is personally made by Bruce to his exacting standards.

L.C.D. screen

MOBILE PHONE and palmtop computer all-in-one, this high-speed processor is encrypted for maximum security. Voice-activated for hands-free use, all calls are "piggy-backed" on WayneTech satellite transmissions and are untraceable.

MENU CALLS

Multi-function keys

Computer mode

MINI MINES
Bruce refined the incendiary ingredients used by the League of Shadows to create an even more powerful percussive explosive. Batman carries these mini mines with both touch-sensitive probes and limited duration timers in addition to the small explosives in his Utility Belt. They are ideal for scuttling pursuing vehicles or blasting out reinforced concrete walls.

*Spikes recessed
for rolling*

*Pressure-sensitive spikes
deployed*

*Arming toggle:
green=unarmed
red=armed*

*Magnetic
attach-point for
grapnel gun*

Quick-release buckle

*Segmented links
distribute weight
supported by belt*

*Antidote ampoules
for Scarecrow's
fear gas*

*Flexible
periscope*

Mobile phone

*Mini
mines*

*Belt grips for
Batarangs*

THE TUMBLER

"Does it come in black?"

With his costume and headquarters completed, Bruce's alter ego is only missing one final thing – a state-of-the-art armoured vehicle. While visiting Lucius Fox, Bruce spies a large and imposing shape under a tarpaulin. Fox reveals a prototype car decked out in desert camouflage paint, a one-of-a-kind military vehicle known affectionately as "the Tumbler".

MILITARY PROTOTYPE
The Tumbler was intended as a bridge-building vehicle to ferry soldiers and supplies across rivers or open spaces such as ravines. Cost overruns and difficulties with the bridge deployment kept the vehicle at the prototype stage.

Thermal-imaging D.V.E.
(Driver's Vision Enhancer)

Halogen spotlights

Blast shutters

Missile launchers

Air-cooled machine guns

Studded spikes extrude for additional traction on slippery or ice-covered roadways

Hoosier self-sealing gel-filled racetrack tyres

Axle-less bolted wheel arm-struts

DESIGNED FOR STEALTH, the Tumbler's angled exterior makes radar tracking difficult. A "silent running" mode can also be activated when the engine switches to electric and the halogen lights are doused. The Tumbler navigates in the dark using technology similar to night-vision goggles.

A **CONVENTIONAL** fuel-injected engine was modified to replace standard military diesel fuel with an experimental high-performance petrol/nitromethane mix. Twin rear-deploying drag-chutes can be used to slow the Tumbler while an inertial reel landing hook facilitates high-speed braking.

REAR VIEW

Forward hydraulic airfoils

Roof-access canopy

Spaced laminate armour

Rear hydraulic airfoils

Quick-stop brake-flaps

4 x 112 cm (44-inch) four-wheel drive Super Swamper tyres

Air intake

Side hydraulic airfoils

Engine noise dampeners

Fuel caps

E.R.A. (Explosive Reactive Armour)

Low-gloss paint

ROCKET FUEL! The Tumbler has a second, higher-powered engine. This jet engine burns liquid propane, providing nearly 1,360 kg (3,000 lbs) of controlled thrust when jumping. The volatile fuel is protected behind conventional armour sheathing and E.R.A. hull-plates, with cut-off switches inside the canopy. If necessary, propane tanks can be jettisoned while the vehicle is travelling at speed.

TUMBLER STATS

LENGTH:	4.5 metres (15 ft)
WIDTH (AT REAR):	2.8 metres (9 ft 4 in)
HEIGHT:	1.6 metres (5 ft 2 in)
WEIGHT:	2.54 tonnes (2.5 tons)
ACCELERATION:	0-60 in 2.9 secs
MAX. SPEED:	322+ km/h (200+ mph)
ENGINE:	1,500 hp jet turbine
FUEL:	Petrol/nitromethane
JET FUEL:	Liquid propane
DRIVE TRAIN:	Rear-wheel drive

MOBILE BAT

The distance from the Batcave to Gotham City center is 19 kilometres (11.9 miles). At top speed, Batman can reach G.C.P.D. headquarters in just under 5 minutes without even engaging the Tumbler's jet afterburners.

THE BATMOBILE

"You should see my other car..."

After putting the Tumbler through its paces on the company's warehouse track, Bruce thinks that his alter ego may just have found the perfect set of wheels for his assault on Gotham City's underworld. Customizing the Tumbler to Bruce's specifications involves a simple-but-crucial alteration – he paints the exterior matte black. Making the armoured and jet-propelled Tumbler stealthier is merely the beginning as Bruce turns this military muscle car into what can only be described as a "Batmobile".

COCKPIT

Redefining the term "state-of-the art technology," the Tumbler's cockpit features one-touch controls for a variety of offensive and defensive measures. Holographic "pop-up" displays replace standard computer screens, optimizing the interior space. The driver and a single passenger will sit comfortably inside the well-protected canopy.

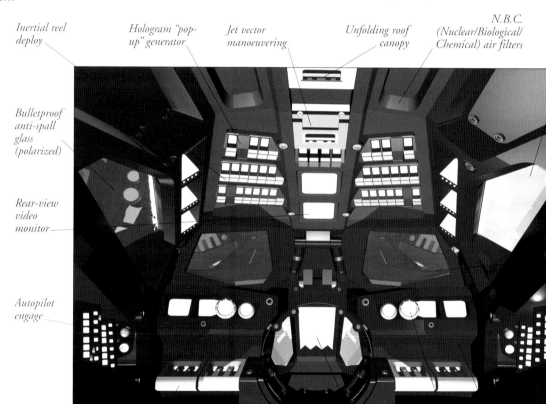

Inertial reel deploy

Hologram "pop-up" generator

Jet vector manoeuvering

Unfolding roof canopy

N.B.C. (Nuclear/Biological/Chemical) air filters

Bulletproof anti-spall glass (un-polarized)

Bulletproof anti-spall glass (polarized)

Rear-view video monitor

Autopilot engage

Sliding armour forward sights

Comms. array

Afterburner toggle

Forward airbags

Impact-resistant plastic

L.C.D. display

Voice-command microphone

Internal speakers

Computer satnav uplink

COCKPIT SEAT

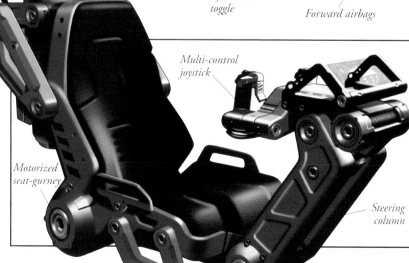

Multi-control joystick

Motorized seat-gurney

Steering column

DRIVER'S SEAT

The gyroscopically balanced seat ensures that the driver remains vertical to the horizontal horizon, no matter what angle the vehicle is at. The motorized, segmented seat tilts and unfolds to allow forward driving, with the pilot lying chest-down for specialized manoeuvres. Satellite navigation ensures that the Tumbler always knows where it is going.

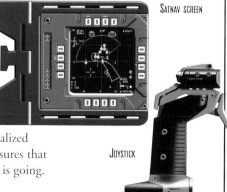

SATNAV SCREEN

JOYSTICK

IN THE FORWARD-SLUNG seat, Batman practises piloting the Tumbler, memorizing every control so that driving the heavily armoured vehicle becomes second nature to him.

MONSTER VEHICLE

Unlike military tanks that simply smash through a barricade with ease, the huge-wheeled Tumbler can also roll over any obstacle, as the G.C.P.D. discovers!

BACK IN THE BATCAVE

The Tumbler's unique features make it the only vehicle able to park in Batman's subterranean headquarters. A natural waterfall conceals an opening large enough for the vehicle to roar right into the Batcave, braking via an inertial reel landing hook which attaches to a steel grommet anchored into the rock floor of the cave.

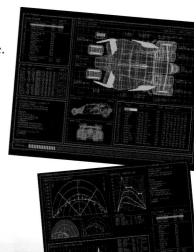

CHECKING SCREENS after a night cruising Gotham's mean streets, Batman monitors the Tumbler's performance. Fuel efficiency and launch vectors are constantly assessed by an onboard computer.

RAMPLESS JUMPING: The Tumbler can jump 1.2-1.8 metres (4-6 feet) up without benefit of a ramp by jamming its airfoils into the air and using its jet-engine for thrust. At maximum speed, this is enough vertical movement for the vehicle to leap in excess of 30 metres (100 feet) without any sort of incline.

BRUCE WAYNE: BILLIONAIRE

—"Turns out you don't actually need a degree to do the international playboy thing."—

Bruce Wayne is as much a carefully constructed mask as Batman's frightening cowl. At Alfred's suggestion, Bruce plays up the persona of a bored socialite with too much time and money on his hands, mostly to explain away the numerous injuries suffered during Batman's nocturnal activities. Bruce feigns just enough interest in Wayne Enterprises to avoid boardroom politics yet take full advantage of the Applied Sciences division. Bruce knows that if Gotham sees him as a playboy, no one will suspect that he is really Batman. And Alfred hopes that a little harmless fun will somehow balance the burden of responsibility Bruce carries on his shoulders.

BRUCE WAYNE'S current favourite car is the Lamborghini Murciélago, with a 12-cylinder V60 engine under the hood and a top speed of 330 km/h (205 mph). It is often described as looking like a bat, an irony not lost on Bruce.

GOTHAM'S V.I.P.

To complete the masquerade of an international playboy, Bruce Wayne must also look the part. He is always immaculately groomed and wears only the finest clothing – tailored suits, Italian shirts, silk ties and handmade shoes. A regular feature of Gotham's gossip columns, it's not uncommon to spot Bruce canoodling with beautiful supermodels or heiresses at the Ritz-Marlton Hotel or the trendy Iceberg Lounge. Wherever he goes, it's understood that Bruce Wayne never has to wait in line and he is not averse to using his loose change to buy anything that takes his fancy, even hotels!

JAMES GORDON

Perhaps it's not surprising that the one decent cop in the G.C.P.D. isn't a native Gothamite. James W. Gordon began his law enforcement career as a lowly beat cop in Chicago. Moving to Gotham with his wife Barbara, Gordon found employment with the G.C.P.D., where his honesty and integrity ran contrary to his hopes of advancement. Gordon's well-deserved promotion to sergeant was a long time coming but unfortunately higher rank brought with it few privileges, especially when Commissioner Loeb partnered him with the slovenly and dishonest Detective Flass. Surrounded by colleagues who flaunt their kickbacks, Jim Gordon feels increasingly jaded and disillusioned. In his heart, Gordon believes in the law and wants Gotham to be a better place for his wife and two young children. But what can one man do? The emergence of the Dark Knight gives Gordon hope for a better Gotham. While he does not condone vigilantes, Gordon begins to see that sometimes operating outside the law is the only way to see justice done in a place like Gotham.

GOTHAM CITY P.D. LOGO

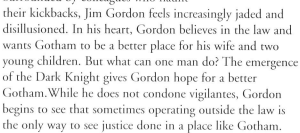

OFFICER JIM GORDON first met Bruce Wayne the night Bruce's parents were murdered. He did his best to console the traumatized youth. Bruce would always remember Gordon's kindness.

FIGHTING BACK
"You're a good cop, one of the few..."

Bruce knows he can't do this alone. Fighting Gotham's criminals is one thing, but making sure that they're punished to the fullest extent of the law is quite another, especially when Carmine Falcone has most of the legal system on his payroll. As he begins his crusade against crime, Bruce recalls a friendly face that gave him hope in the darkest moments of his childhood. This is the man to help him clean up Gotham. They will start with Falcone and his drug smuggling ring.

NOW WE ARE TWO

Working late in his cramped office, Gordon is surprised by a masked intruder pressing what feels like the barrel of a gun into his back. In fact, Bruce Wayne uses a stapler to keep Gordon's attention as he questions him about Falcone's drug smuggling and the police's inability to stop the notorious crimelord. After getting the information he needs, Bruce tells Gordon to wait for a sign and slips out. Gun drawn, Gordon races out of the building after his visitor, but Bruce escapes easily.

ASSISTANT DISTRICT ATTORNEY

Rachel Dawes is suspicious of Dr Crane's motives for declaring Victor Zsaz insane so she confronts him outside the court. Zsaz joins a growing list of violent criminals and thugs with ties to mobster Carmine Falcone who are remanded to Crane's care at Arkham Asylum, thanks to Judge Faden. Rachel accuses Crane of corruption, until her boss, D.A. Carl Finch, advises her to be more cautious.

BATMAN STRIKES

Batman makes his first public appearance at the Gotham docks. As a shipment arrives, he discovers that Falcone is smuggling narcotics inside stuffed toys. With Detective Flass providing police "protection", Falcone himself is overseeing the distribution of the teddy bears and rabbits. Both men are caught by surprise as Batman waylays Falcone's thugs one-by-one. Screams echo through the corridors of shipping containers as Batman makes his terrifying presence known.

SURROUNDED by Falcone's hired muscle, Batman shatters the dock lights with a well-aimed Batarang to even the odds. Fighting blindly in the darkness, the thugs are now in Batman's element.

FALCONE'S FATE

With his bodyguards out for the count, Carmine Falcone is reluctant to leave his limousine but Batman has other plans. The cops arrive just in time to see the silhouette of a bat filling the sky. At the source of the light, Gordon finds an unconscious Falcone all ready to be taken into custody.

READ ALL ABOUT IT! Gotham's newspapers have a field day as headlines proclaim the news of Falcone's capture by the mysterious "Bat-Man" and the mobster's embarrassing moment in the spotlight.

THE SCARECROW

"Would you like to see my mask?"

Carmine Falcone's drug ring is merely the tip of the iceberg; a larger and more insidious plot is yet to be uncovered. Batman is certain of one thing – Jonathan Crane's involvement in this secret scheme goes far beyond his alliance with Falcone. In fact, Batman will discover that both Crane and Falcone are in league with a third, more dangerous foe, whose identity and sinister motivations will soon be revealed.

WITH THE TERRIFYING mask and a hangman's noose around his neck, Dr Jonathan Crane becomes the fearsome Scarecrow.

FALCONE IS GASSED

Jonathan Crane has been paid handsomely to keep guilty men out of jail. All they needed to do was feign a little mental unbalance in front of a "kindly" judge and they would be sent to Arkham instead. Following his arrest Falcone does the same, but Falcone and Crane's secret partner wants to ensure that the mob boss cannot reveal his identity. While evaluating Falcone, Crane dons the Scarecrow mask and gasses him with a toxin that makes the mobster see his worst fears brought to life. After inhaling Crane's fear gas, Falcone no longer needs to fake raving lunacy.

FEAR 101

As a child, Jonathan Crane was bullied in school by classmates who cruelly dubbed the skinny and awkward boy "The Scarecrow". Although frightened by his tormentors, Crane came to realize that his nickname could become the embodiment of fear. His interest in the subject of fear developed into an obsession with understanding phobias and the body's chemical reactions to being frightened. Crane took his study of fear too far at Gotham University and his tenure was revoked for endangering students with his unorthodox experiments. However, he managed to secure a position as administrator of Arkham Asylum where the insane provide ideal guinea pigs. To finance new experiments in fear, Crane has gone into business with Carmine Falcone and someone who supplies him with the key ingredient to finally perfect his fear gas.

THE GOOD DOCTOR

DANGEROUS TOYS

Anyone who intercepted Falcone's shipment would easily uncover the narcotics hidden within the stuffing. However, the toys also conceal another dangerous substance. Virtually indistinguishable from the drugs is the distillation of a rare blue poppy that grows only in the highest and coldest regions of the Himalayas. This secret ingredient is part of a grander scheme concocted by Crane's secret partner. After Falcone is arrested, Crane makes certain that the smuggled narcotics are safely delivered to a rundown apartment in the Narrows.

THE MICROWAVE EMITTER

Designed and built by Wayne Industries, the Microwave Emitter is so top secret, its creation is known only to the highest-level Wayne Enterprises employees. Even Lucius Fox does not know of its existence until Earle informs him that it has been stolen! Other experimental H.P.M. (High-Powered Microwave) devices have been developed by military contractors to interrupt enemy radio communications by releasing a focused transient energy wave. In contrast, the Microwave Emitter was envisioned for desert warfare, targeting an enemy's water supply and vaporizing it with a microwave pulse and turning liquid directly to gas.

Casing closed for transport

Retractable handles

Locking mechanisms at seam-points

CLOSED CASING

CASING MECHANISM OPEN

Microwave radiation shielding

Hydraulic extenders open M.E. to firing position

Focused microwave pulse generator

"Faraday Cage" protects M.E. circuits from the weapon itself

Thumbprint-scan security measure

The Microwave Emitter is no larger than a small refrigerator.

DOWN THE DRAIN goes the powdered distillate smuggled inside the stuffed rabbits. Under Dr Crane's supervision, the patients at Arkham Asylum, including Victor Zsaz, pour the secret substance into a cistern beneath Arkham, mixing it with the water drunk by every Gotham citizen!

FEAR FACTOR

—"There was something else in the drugs, something hidden..."—

Batman's first meeting with Detective Flass left a lasting impression on the crooked cop. Encountering the Dark Knight for a second time on the streets of Gotham, Flass needs very little persuasion to reveal the destination of Falcone's drugs Flass points Batman in the direction of the Narrows, to a single ghetto tenement in particular. There the Dark Knight gets his first experience of fear gas from the Scarecrow!

FINDING THE STUFFED rabbits, Batman realizes that whatever secrets the toys contained have already been removed. When he hears a noise at the door, Batman melts into the shadows of the seedy apartment.

SCAREDY BAT

As he scales the walls of the tenement building, the Dark Knight meets a helpful young boy. He gives the boy his periscope to prove that he has met Batman. Later, as Crane and a pair of thugs return to burn any incriminating evidence, Batman is forced into close-quarters conflict. Stealing away to the apartment's bathroom, Batman surprises one gun-wielding thug before dispatching the second henchman. But Crane gets the upper hand, attacking Batman with a puff of his patented fear gas!

FIRE! Caught in the throes of terrifying hallucinations, Batman is helpless as the Scarecrow splashes him with petrol and sets him on fire. Although his Nomex suit protects him from the flames, Batman suffers waking nightmares from the fear gas. Disorientated, he lurches toward the window and leaps!

UNABLE TO to deploy his glider-cape, Batman spirals to the ground. The hard landing brings him to his senses and he is able to call Alfred before the gas forces him to relive his childhood fall down the well.

IN SAFE HANDS

Barely conscious when Alfred arrives to collect him, Bruce has just enough wits left to tell his faithful valet to take a sample of his poisoned blood. When Bruce wakes up two days later, he discovers that he owes his health and sanity to Lucius Fox, who synthesized an antidote for the fear toxin after Alfred alerted him to Bruce's critical condition.

THE ANTIDOTE

BATMAN TO THE RESCUE

"Who knows you're here?"

THE ONLY WORD Rachel can distinguish in Falcone's insane mutterings is "Scarecrow". She is determined to ask Dr Crane what it means.

A rematch between Batman and Scarecrow is inevitable, especially when Bruce learns that Rachel Dawes has gone to Arkham to confront Dr Crane. Upon hearing that Falcone is on suicide watch at Arkham, a suspicious Rachel undertakes an after-hours fact-finding mission, alone. After surviving one attempt on her life, Rachel doesn't realize that she may be walking into a trap. However, a Dark Knight with matte black armour will be watching over Rachel tonight…

FRIGHTENED out of her wits by a dose of fear gas, Rachel is interrogated by the evil doctor and his henchmen. But as Rachel writhes in panicked delirium, Crane and his thugs will soon experience real fear when they come face-to-face with Rachel's self-appointed protector – Batman!

THE FEAR gas will not affect Batman this time, thanks to Fox's antidote. Little does he know that Rachel is already under its influence.

SCARE TACTICS

Knowing the ineptitude of the G.C.P.D., Crane hopes they will do his dirty work for him and calls them to report a caped intruder. And while the Dark Knight is preoccupied with taking out Crane's thugs, Crane dons his Scarecrow mask and tries to give Batman another dose of fear gas! Unaffected, Batman overpowers the Scarecrow and removes his mask.

THE S.W.A.T. team only complicate matters as they have strict orders from Commissioner Loeb to shoot Batman on sight!

GOTHAM S.W.A.T. TEAM
The Special Weapons and Tactics team are usually called upon for hostage negotiations, officer-down rescues, and school disaster responses. Each team member is qualified in a variety of firearms, including .223 caliber sniper rifles and MP5SD6 semiautomatics with laser-sights.

SWAT
S.W.A.T. TEAM LOGO

AS BATMAN forces Crane to inhale his own fear gas, Crane sees Batman's cowl as a death mask. Terrified, he reveals who he works for – Rā's al Ghūl! Rā's is dead, surely Crane is delirious?

RESCUING RACHEL isn't easy, especially when the Scarecrow's fear gas makes her see Batman as a winged demon! As Rachel lashes out at him, the Dark Knight has no choice but to apply a nerve pinch to Rachel's neck, rendering her unconscious and ready for transport.

POLICE PROTECTION

As S.W.A.T. teams seal off the Asylum, Batman is trapped inside. He finds Jim Gordon and explains that time is running out for Rachel – if she doesn't receive the antidote to the fear toxin soon, the damage to her psyche will be permanent! Gordon agrees to escort Rachel to a side-exit while Batman calls for back-up. Using the sonic sounder in his boot, Batman calls swarms of bats to swoop down on the S.W.A.T. cops and conceal his escape.

A CHASE begins as Batman bundles Rachel into the Tumbler and races away. Determined to get Rachel to safety, the Dark Knight won't let anyone stop him. He easily outpaces the G.C.P.D. in his jet-propelled vehicle, as the fearful Rachel clings on for dear life. Police roadblocks can't stop him, as the Tumbler rolls over and smashes through police cars blocking its path! With a final burst of speed, the Tumbler melts into the night.

BACK IN THE BATCAVE, Batman administers the antidote to Rachel. As she slowly recovers, the Dark Knight gives her additional samples of the anti-toxin – one for Jim Gordon and the rest to begin synthesizing additional antidotes. Unfortunately, Batman fears that the threat to Gotham is just beginning…

BIRTHDAY PARTY

—"There's somebody here you simply must meet…"—

Celebrating was the last thing on Bruce's mind – he would rather devote his energies to trying to foil Crane's plot to flood Gotham with fear gas. After leaving Rachel to recuperate under Alfred's care in the safety of the Batcave, Bruce ascends the secret passage to find his birthday party already in full swing. Alas, even the best parties can be ruined by gatecrashers. An uninvited guest is about to reveal that Batman's true enemy is not Falcone or even Crane, but a familiar face who is far more dangerous.

BRUCE'S PARTY takes place in his lavishly decorated ballroom. In addition to Wayne Enterprises' board of directors and staff, a who's who of Gotham's rich and famous make appearances to honour the city's favourite prodigal son.

FOX REVEALS to Bruce what he has discovered about the Microwave Emitter. Bruce has an even bigger problem than he thought!

THE SECRET REVEALED

Bruce is shocked when a guest introduces him to a Mr Al Ghūl, but the man wearing a blue poppy in his lapel is not the leader of the League of Shadows. Confused, Bruce turns to find Henri Ducard. Slowly the truth dawns on him – Ducard is Rā's al Ghūl! The man who taught Bruce the subtle arts of the ninja has tricked him all along. Worse still, Bruce now realizes the identity of the mysterious malefactor behind Crane's fear gas and the plot to destroy Gotham!

MANOR IN FLAMES

Bruce sees that a dozen ninjas have taken up positions throughout his party. To spare the guests' lives, Bruce feigns a drunken tirade, insulting his guests so that they leave. Rā's al Ghūl wants retribution for the destruction of his monastery so he orders his men to set Wayne Manor ablaze. Rā's al Ghūl then unsheathes a sword hidden in his cane, leaving Bruce for dead as the Manor is consumed by flames.

WIELDING BRUCE'S nine iron golf club as a handy cudgel, Alfred knocks a gun-toting warrior unconscious! He will do anything his power to protect Bruce from harm.

As BRUCE LIES trapped beneath burning timbers, Alfred knows he isn't strong enough to shift the heavy beam. With a hard slap to rouse Bruce, Alfred spurs him to action. Bruce frees himself, and, with Alfred propping him up, limps to the secret entrance to the Batcave as Wayne Manor disintegrates around them!

ALFRED BINDS Bruce's wounds and reminds him that the Wayne legacy is more than just bricks and mortar. Bruce finds renewed resolve in Alfred's wise words: Batman must stop Rā's al Ghūl!

TERROR IN THE NARROWS

"How many were in maximum security?"

The inmates are in control of the Asylum! Before Rā's al Ghūl left him for dead, Bruce learned that the League of Shadows has infiltrated nearly every level of Gotham, even the G.C.P.D. Unbeknownst to Jim Gordon, ninjas disguised as S.W.A.T. cops create chaos in the Narrows while their master hurries to unleash the Scarecrow's fear gas on Gotham – using the the Microwave Emitter stolen from Wayne Enterprises!

THE ARKHAM BREAKOUT is organized by the phoney S.W.A.T. cops. The League of Shadows turns the Asylum inmates loose from their cells and use explosives to blow open a gaping whole for the maniacs and murderers to step through Arkham's walls. Among the escapees is serial killer Mr Zsaz!

THE PLOT THICKENS

Rā's al Ghūl's plan is to choke Gotham with the hallucinogenic fear toxin which has already been added to the city's water supply. To do this he needs to turn the water into a gas, which is simple, thanks to the Microwave Emitter. Rā's begins in the Narrows, blowing the water mains sky-high. As the pressure causes the pipes to burst, manhole covers rocket into the air. The water turns to vapour and fear gas covers the Narrows in a toxic fog, turning a bad situation into the very worst-case scenario.

RĀ'S AND HIS minions don gas masks to spare them from the effects of the fear gas.

RACHEL and the boy who met Batman in the Narrows are caught up in the mayhem, unaware that the S.W.A.T. cops are working for Rā's al Ghūl!

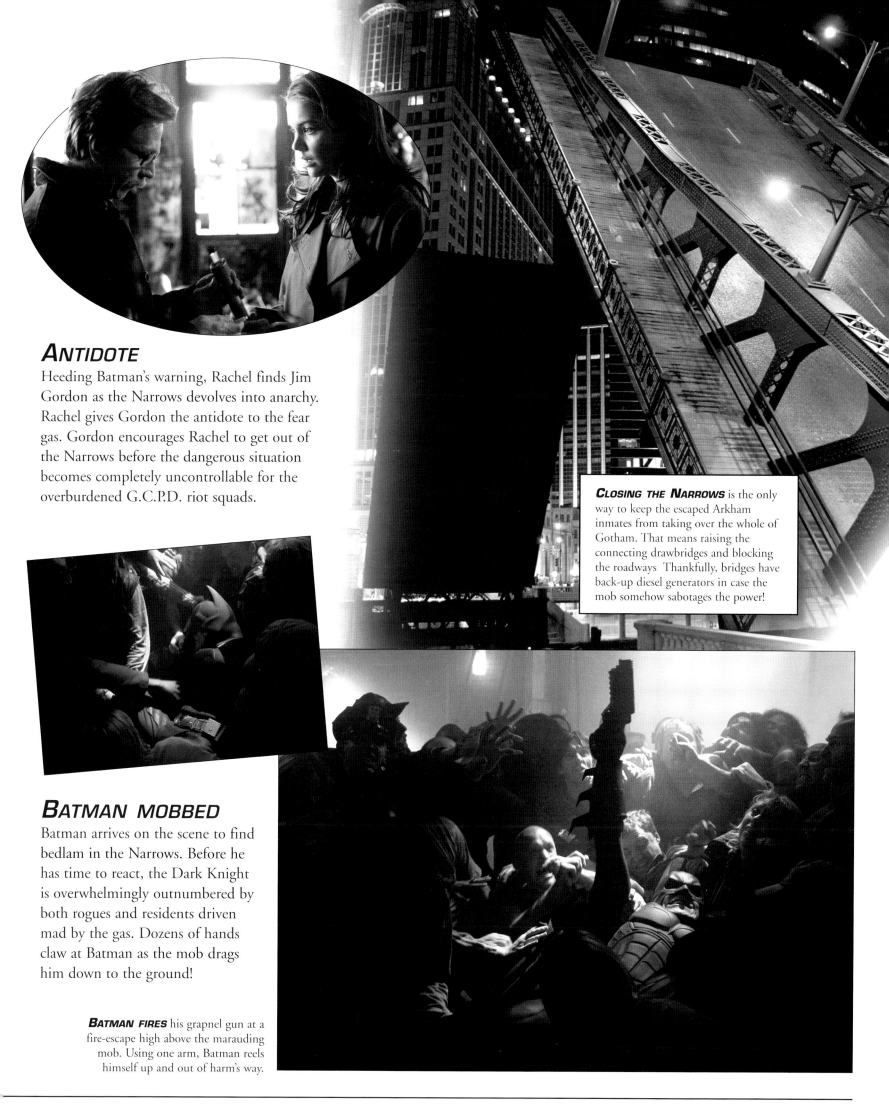

ANTIDOTE

Heeding Batman's warning, Rachel finds Jim Gordon as the Narrows devolves into anarchy. Rachel gives Gordon the antidote to the fear gas. Gordon encourages Rachel to get out of the Narrows before the dangerous situation becomes completely uncontrollable for the overburdened G.C.P.D. riot squads.

CLOSING THE NARROWS is the only way to keep the escaped Arkham inmates from taking over the whole of Gotham. That means raising the connecting drawbridges and blocking the roadways Thankfully, bridges have back-up diesel generators in case the mob somehow sabotages the power!

BATMAN MOBBED

Batman arrives on the scene to find bedlam in the Narrows. Before he has time to react, the Dark Knight is overwhelmingly outnumbered by both rogues and residents driven mad by the gas. Dozens of hands claw at Batman as the mob drags him down to the ground!

BATMAN FIRES his grapnel gun at a fire-escape high above the marauding mob. Using one arm, Batman reels himself up and out of harm's way.

BATMAN WINS

–"Have you finally learned to do what's necessary?"–

The chaos in the Narrows is just the beginning for Rā's al Ghūl. With the majority of the city's police and emergency-response teams busy sealing off the Narrows so that no one can get in or out by roadway, Rā's al Ghūl has already departed via monorail. As the train speeds toward the heart of Gotham, Rā's al Ghūl uses the Microwave Emitter to release the fear gas once again. Batman and Gordon are in hot pursuit, while Rachel has to defend herself against a familiar masked horseman… The Scarecrow!

SHOCK THERAPY!
Rachel fires her taser straight at the Crane, shooting volts of electricity between the eyeholes of the Scarecrow mask.

THE SCARECROW is a fearsome figure in the saddle of a mounted policeman's steed, the horse's former master dragging behind it by one of the stirrups.

THE DARK KNIGHT appears in the nick of time! Her taser-charge spent, Rachel is defenseless as Mr Zsaz and the Arkham lunatics converge on them. At that moment, Batman swoops in and lifts Rachel and the boy out of harm's way, using his grapnel gun. Safe on a rooftop, Rachel finally realizes who her masked saviour really is.

FRIGHTENED AWAY

Driven insane by his own fear gas, Dr Crane found himself straitjacketed after his second encounter with Batman. However, he was freed by League of Shadows warriors disguised as S.W.A.T. cops. After Batman prevents the Scarecrow from terrorizing Rachel Dawes in the Narrows, Crane slips away in the ensuing chaos. He remains at large.

WITH RACHEL safe Batman uses another well-aimed grapnel to catch the train carrying Rā's al Ghūl and the Microwave Emitter. He has to hang on for dear life as the monorail roars out of the Narrows trailing steam-burst fire hydrants in its wake. Slowly the Dark Knight reels himself closer to the train, with all of Gotham depending on him.

ENTRUSTED WITH THE Tumbler by Batman, Jim Gordon can't wait to get behind the wheel – how hard can it be? Confused by the complex controls, Gordon takes a while to figure out the vehicle's brakes from its accelerator and as he speeds off, the Batmobile accidentally sideswipes a few parked cars. But Batman needs all the help he can get in the race to save Gotham!

BREAKING THE SPEED LIMIT, Gordon races to stop the monorail. But he is unsure of Batman's progress in climbing aboard the seemingly runaway train – if the Dark Knight is unsuccessful, the whole of Gotham will soon be feeling the effects of the fear toxin. Rocketing ahead of the train, Gordon aims straight for one of the monorail's concrete support columns. Without a moment's hesitation, he fires a volley of missiles from the Batmobile to give the train nowhere else to go but down!

FINAL BATTLE

As the monorail zooms out of control, Batman realizes its final destination – Wayne Tower! That is where the control room of the city's water board is located and if the Microwave Emitter reaches there it will vaporize the entire city's water supply and flood Gotham with fear gas! Clambering aboard the train, Batman faces his former mentor as Rā's al Ghūl draws his sword. But the Dark Knight has learned some new tricks since the two men last fought. In a ferocious fight, Batman uses his gauntlets to tear Rā's al Ghūl's sword in two. As he gains the upper hand, Batman sees that Gordon has destroyed the monorail support ahead!

"I WON'T KILL YOU" whispers Batman, "But I don't have to save you." As the train crashes, Batman escapes and leaves Rā's al Ghūl to his fate.

THE FIGHT CONTINUES

"You've started something..."

CONTROLLING INTEREST in Wayne Enterprises is secured by Bruce Wayne when he purchases the majority of the company's recently floated shares. Earle is replaced as C.E.O. by Lucius Fox. With Fox at the helm, Bruce knows that his family business is once more in good hands.

Rā's al Ghūl is presumed dead, but as the League of Shadows leader's body has not been recovered, Bruce can't help wondering whether their duel might continue in another time and place. For Bruce's alter ego, this is merely the end of his first chapter; Batman's work is only just beginning. The good people of Gotham City can allow themselves to hope at last – a Dark Knight will be keeping watch over them. The bad people of Gotham City had better watch out...

MANOR IN RUINS

After his parents' deaths, Bruce described Wayne Manor as a mausoleum, vowing to tear it down brick by brick. The League of Shadows very nearly accomplished that for him, but like its master, the Manor's foundation stands strong. With Alfred's help, Bruce vows to rebuild his family home.

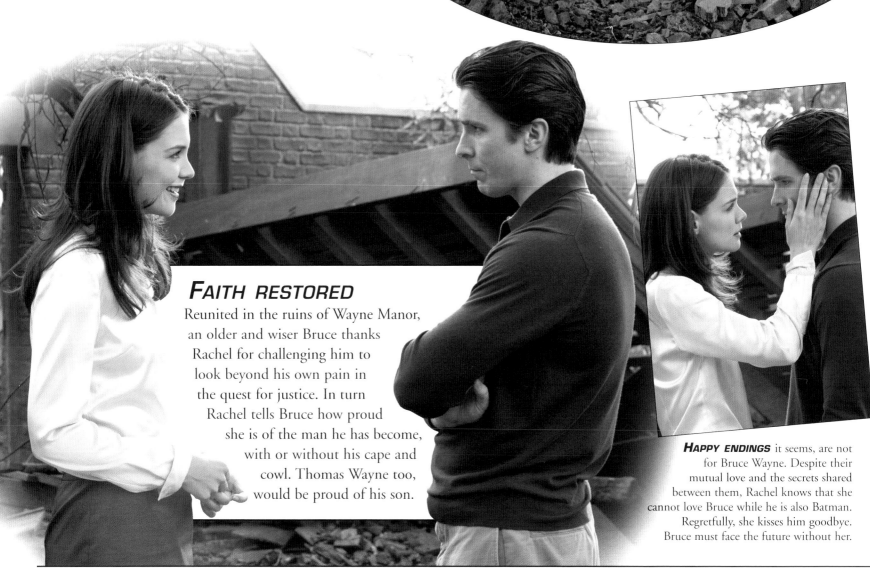

FAITH RESTORED

Reunited in the ruins of Wayne Manor, an older and wiser Bruce thanks Rachel for challenging him to look beyond his own pain in the quest for justice. In turn Rachel tells Bruce how proud she is of the man he has become, with or without his cape and cowl. Thomas Wayne too, would be proud of his son.

HAPPY ENDINGS it seems, are not for Bruce Wayne. Despite their mutual love and the secrets shared between them, Rachel knows that she cannot love Bruce while he is also Batman. Regretfully, she kisses him goodbye. Bruce must face the future without her.

UNEASY ALLIANCE

Jim Gordon's involvement in saving Gotham results in his promotion to the rank of lieutenant. The G.C.P.D. is still mired in corruption, but Gordon is determined to clean it up from within. He has developed a Bat-Signal to summon the Caped Crusader in times of need. Gotham is calm now, but both men know that the war on crime has begun in earnest. And with a tentative trust forged between them, Batman and Gordon will fight it together.

THE LAST LAUGH may yet go to the villains. Whether unleashed by Crane's fear gas or enticed by Batman's spreading legend, the deranged of Gotham are on the move. Batman's next big case? It could be an armed robber who murders with glee and leaves this calling card at the scenes of his crimes…

THE BAT-SIGNAL

ACKNOWLEDGEMENTS

THE AUTHOR WOULD LIKE TO THANK THE FOLLOWING FOR THEIR INVALUABLE HELP IN PRODUCING THIS BOOK:

Steve Korté, Catherine Saunders, Christopher Nolan, Emma Thomas,
David Goyer, Shane Thompson, Susannah Scott, Irika Slavin, Melissa Miller,
Mick Mayhew, Paul Levitz, Chris Cerasi, Rob Perry, Alex Allen, Dennis O'Neil,
Linda Fields, Jaye Gardner, Kilian Plunkett, and Jennifer Myskowski.

THE PUBLISHER WOULD ALSO LIKE TO THANK THE FOLLOWING:

Julia March for proofreading assistance and Mika Kean-Hammerson for design assistance.